U.S.-Japan Alliance Conference

The U.S.-Japan Alliance in an Era of Strategic Competition

JEFFREY W. HORNUNG

Sponsored by the Government of Japan

For more information on this publication, visit **www.rand.org/t/CFA2839-1**.

About RAND

The RAND Corporation is a research organization that develops solutions to public policy challenges to help make communities throughout the world safer and more secure, healthier and more prosperous. RAND is nonprofit, nonpartisan, and committed to the public interest. To learn more about RAND, visit www.rand.org.

Research Integrity

Our mission to help improve policy and decisionmaking through research and analysis is enabled through our core values of quality and objectivity and our unwavering commitment to the highest level of integrity and ethical behavior. To help ensure our research and analysis are rigorous, objective, and nonpartisan, we subject our research publications to a robust and exacting quality-assurance process; avoid both the appearance and reality of financial and other conflicts of interest through staff training, project screening, and a policy of mandatory disclosure; and pursue transparency in our research engagements through our commitment to the open publication of our research findings and recommendations, disclosure of the source of funding of published research, and policies to ensure intellectual independence. For more information, visit www.rand.org/about/principles.

RAND's publications do not necessarily reflect the opinions of its research clients and sponsors.

Published by the RAND Corporation, Santa Monica, Calif.

Library of Congress Cataloging-in-Publication Data is available for this publication.
ISBN: 978-1-9774-1225-6

Cover image adapted from blackred/Getty Images and Allexxandar/Getty Images.

About These Conference Proceedings

Key U.S. allies are looking at the war in Ukraine to draw lessons for their security planning, a trend that has opened new opportunities for the United States and Japan to expand and deepen their security ties with one another. To assess the implications of the war in Ukraine on the Indo-Pacific region and the lessons that today's conflict may portend for the U.S.-Japan alliance, the RAND Corporation organized a pair of virtual conferences in fall 2022. These proceedings contain a summary of those conferences and an analytical assessment based on those conferences.

RAND National Security Research Division

This research exchange was sponsored by the Government of Japan and conducted within the International Security and Defense Policy Center of the RAND National Security Research Division (NSRD). NSRD conducts research and analysis for the Office of the Secretary of Defense, the U.S. Intelligence Community, the U.S. State Department, allied foreign governments, and foundations.

For more information on the RAND International Security and Defense Policy Center, see www.rand.org/nsrd/isdp or contact the director (contact information is provided on the webpage).

Acknowledgments

These conference proceedings benefited from helpful reviews by RAND Corporation colleague Kristen Gunness and by Zack Cooper of the American Enterprise Institute. The author would also like to thank RAND colleague Naoko Aoki, who summarized the contents of the two online sessions. Finally, a special thank you to the four gentlemen of the Institute of Global Politics who provided critical research inputs to the analytical portion of these conference proceedings.

Contents

CHAPTER 1

Introduction

Russia's war against Ukraine shocked the world both in terms of its naked aggression and brutality. Aside from the hostilities themselves, Russian aggression has sparked conversations about a similar war being started by other major powers in other parts of the world. In particular, given China's persistent claim that Taiwan is a breakaway province and the history of Chinese provocations directed at Taiwan, comparisons are naturally drawn between Russia's aggression and possible Chinese kinetic military action against Taiwan. These comparisons, in turn, elicit several important questions for the United States and its ally Japan. How difficult would it be for the United States and Japan to assemble an international coalition to counter Chinese military action? What lessons from Ukraine's defensive operations are applicable to the United States and Japan in a potential war in Northeast Asia? In which areas should the allies focus their attention? Can anything be done in peacetime to deter China from starting armed conflict in the region? What types of strategic lessons are Japan and the United States drawing from the war in Europe to protect and preserve the liberal international order? What are the potential implications of the war in Ukraine for the U.S.-Japan alliance?

To explore these questions, the RAND Corporation convened a pair of virtual conferences that brought together experts on Europe, Japan, Taiwan, and U.S. security policies in fall 2022 to explore issues of relevance to the U.S.-Japan alliance with respect to the era of strategic competition. These conference proceedings capture the insights that the experts developed in their presentations and include a short analytical portion based on these insights.

Conference One: The Impact of the War in Ukraine on the Indo-Pacific Region

The first conference, held on September 15, 2022, focused on the impact of the war in Ukraine on the Indo-Pacific region. Keynote remarks were delivered at the event by the Honorable Harry Harris, a former U.S. Ambassador to South Korea and a retired admiral in the U.S. Navy, where he served for 40 years. The focus of Harris's remarks was extremely relevant to tying together both the current war in the Ukraine and a hypothetical war in two different parts of the world and laying out the implications for the U.S.-Japan alliance at the same time. Noting that the world is potentially at an inflection point in which freedom, justice, and the rules-based system hang in the balance, Harris noted three countries that pose considerable challenge to the Indo-Pacific region: North Korea, China, and Russia. Given these challenges, Harris argued for the continued importance of diplomacy and the U.S. regional alliance system, including the U.S.-Japan alliance. Drawing connections between today's war in Ukraine and a possible war over Taiwan, Harris spoke about the lessons Indo-Pacific countries could draw from Russia's invasion of Ukraine and the lessons the United States could draw on as it pertains to building coalitions in the Indo-Pacific to push back on aggression. Looking at Ukraine's defense operations against Russia, Harris drew comparisons with the East China Sea to note challenges to logistic operations in a conflict over Taiwan. Harris also referenced the troubling nature of the strengthening bilateral ties between China and Russia, such as China aligning with Russia on the Ukraine war. Finally, echoing a broader debate in the United States about the best policy a U.S. President should pursue regarding Taiwan, Harris spoke at length about the need for strategic clarity regarding U.S. policy vis-à-vis Taiwan. In particular, Harris cautioned that Russia took advantage of the U.S. declaratory policy of sending no troops to Ukraine. Harris said that, because China has been clear on its intent regarding Taiwan, the United States should itself provide greater clarity on its intentions. The panel discussion that followed touched on similar themes.

The first presenter, Abiru Taisuke of Sasakawa Peace Foundation, set the context for understanding Japan's policies by noting that Japan's response to the Russian invasion of Ukraine marked a shift in its long-standing policy toward Russia. Responding to the infringement on Ukraine's sovereignty and territorial integrity, the administration of Japanese Prime Minister Kishida Fumio not only provided aid packages to Ukraine but also imposed an unprecedented level of economic sanctions against Russia. Abiru said that Tokyo shifted its policy for three reasons: the seriousness of Russia's invasion merited a harsher response, the stalled negotiations between Japan and Russia made a peace treaty unlikely, and there was a need to send a message to China that it should not try to change the status quo by force. Although he believed that the Kishida administration made the right choice in supporting Ukraine, Abiru noted strategic implications that the U.S.-Japan alliance need to consider. For example, Russia is likely to be weakened because of the war in Ukraine and, therefore, will likely increase its dependence on China, leading Japan to face not just the strategic challenges from China and North Korea but also a potentially hostile Russia.

Dara Massicot, senior policy researcher at the RAND Corporation, gave the second presentation, explaining there were two early takeaways from the war in Ukraine (as of fall 2022). The first concerned how Ukraine, a highly motivated country with a will to fight, was able to rapidly absorb training and military equipment during the crisis. Massicot argued that this will affect U.S. thinking about how to support allies and partners in the Indo-Pacific region during a possible crisis there, such as over Taiwan. A second takeaway from the Ukraine war was the intense rate of equipment and munitions expenditure. Massicot said that the high rate showed that the U.S. defense industrial base is not constructed to produce at the pace needed for a high-intensity war, which could have implications for a crisis in the Indo-Pacific area. Finally, on broader geopolitical implications for the Indo-Pacific region, Massicot thought that U.S. support of Ukraine sent a deterrent message around the world to those who seek to change borders by force. Importantly, Massicot did not foresee a need to shift U.S. capabilities from the Indo-Pacific region to Europe to help the war effort in Ukraine because of key differences in the theaters. The capabilities needed for the ground war in Europe are different from the types of assets that would be needed in an airborne and maritime Indo-Pacific conflict.

The final presenter was Michael Mazarr, senior political scientist at the RAND Corporation. In speaking about the broad geopolitical consequences of the war, Mazarr argued that the day Russia invaded Ukraine may eventually be seen as a high watermark for the geopolitical standing of China and Russia. Mazarr noted that, although the common perception is that the world is undergoing a power transition in which China is overtaking the United States, he thought the opposite could be true. Based on this opinion, Mazarr said that the world may be heading toward a more multipolar system in which the United States is still the first among equals that coordinates among a group of industrial democracies, status quo powers, and emerging market countries, all of which favor a stable world system.

Conference Two: The View of the Taiwan Strait from the U.S.-Japan Alliance

The second conference, convened on October 10, 2022, focused on the view of the Taiwan Strait from the U.S.-Japan alliance. Providing this event's keynote speech was Matthew Pottinger, former U.S. Deputy National Security Advisor and former Senior Director for Asia on the National Security Council. In his remarks, Pottinger argued that for free and open societies to survive and prosper, they must win the war in Ukraine and deter a war in Taiwan. Pottinger argued that, because countries go to war because of optimism that they can achieve more through war than through diplomacy, the United States and Japan should do everything they can to dampen China's optimistic belief that a war over Taiwan would be successful. Toward that end, he advised that Japan and the United States, together with other allies and partners, should state more clearly their intentions to fight if Beijing tries to invade Taiwan. Pottinger looked to the war in Ukraine and highlighted two lessons for Taiwan: the importance of the will to fight and the difficulty in resupplying. Finally, referring to the late Japanese Prime Minister Abe Shinzō's vision of the free and open Indo-Pacific, Pottinger argued the United States, Japan, and other like-minded partners need to work together and perhaps clarify intent regarding their positions over Taiwan. According to Pottinger, this is important because it would be extremely difficult for China to succeed in a conflict over Taiwan if Japan were to enter the war with the United States. The panel discussion that followed touched on similar themes.

The first presenter was Cortez Cooper, a senior defense researcher at the RAND Corporation. Cooper argued that Taiwan can be the proximate cause for a major power conflict involving China and the United States. Cooper said that the United States and its allies and partners, such as Japan, need to think about how to respond to the increase in Chinese coercive activities against Taiwan, especially because China could try to normalize coercive behavior. Cooper argued that Taiwan is important for the United States for three primary reasons. First, Taiwan is the critical link in the First Island Chain running from Japan through the Philippines to the South China Sea, which are major sea lines of trade and communication. Second, Taiwan is an important economy that produces critical products, such as high-end semiconductors. Finally, Taiwan is a beacon of democracy, which should be a concern not just for the United States but also for allies, such as Japan. Cooper also noted that, although the United States is concerned about whether it can deter China from attacking Taiwan, China believes that it is becoming increasingly difficult to deter the United States from reinforcing Taiwan in ways that would lead to the island's permanent separation or independence, a situation he referred to as a *deterrence dilemma*.

The second presenter was Matsuda Yasuhiro of the University of Tokyo, who focused on the views of Taiwan in Japan. Matsuda argued that both ordinary citizens and political elites are concerned about the tensions over Taiwan, with some worrying that China could take extreme actions if the country's economy deteriorates. He argued that China is dealing with two contradictory wishes: (1) It does not want to provoke the United States and its allies, but (2) it wants to intimidate Taiwan. Matsuda said that, although Japan's policy on Taiwan has not changed and Japan has maintained nongovernmental relations with Taiwan, affinity between the people of Japan and Taiwan has grown. Matsuda thought this meant that although the Japanese government cannot promote political relations with Taiwan, it cannot treat Taiwan lightly either, as there could be repercussions from both the right and left political wings in Japan. Matsuda also said that Taiwan is the cornerstone of the international order in the region, and if China succeeds in taking it by force, Pax Americana in the region will end. He went on to argue that if the United States chooses to not intervene in a Taiwan contingency, the U.S.-Japan alliance will no longer function, as Japan will lose faith in it. Finally, Matsuda noted that, although it is out of the question for

Japan to declare that it will defend Taiwan, Japan could defend itself, which, through continuing efforts to strengthen its own defense capabilities, can contribute to deterring China's aggression more broadly speaking.

The final presentation was provided by Sheila Smith, the John E. Merow Senior Fellow for Asia-Pacific Studies at the Council on Foreign Relations. Smith argued that there were three changes to the Taiwan situation that make policymaking challenging for both the United States and Japan. The first was the change in the military balance between the United States and China. Smith said that although the United States had been confident of its own military dominance in the past, it is less so today. The second was the fact that the pathways to solve problems between the United States and China have narrowed considerably. Finally, Smith noted that tensions over Taiwan were taking place at a time of major power competition. This factor means that Taiwan is not only a regional issue or a residual Cold War flash-point but a potential trigger for a major power war. Together, Smith argued the postwar rules-based order is being fundamentally challenged.

In the spirit of these two conferences, the next section presents an analysis that seeks to address some of the lessons learned from the war in Ukraine and the implications for the U.S.-Japan alliance regarding a possible Chinese invasion of Taiwan. An important note to readers: Because the virtual conferences were held in fall 2022, some of the content by the presenters may not reflect the realities of the security situation in Europe and the strategic priorities of the actors examined in their discussions. For the full conference, please watch the videos at the following online locations:

- The September 15, 2022, conference: Harry B. Harris, Jr., Taisuke Abiru, Dara Massicot, Michael J. Mazarr, Kenko Sone, and Jeffrey W. Hornung, *The Impact of the War in Ukraine on the Indo-Pacific Region*, RAND Corporation, CF-A2070-3, 2022, www.rand.org/t/CFA2070-3.
- The October 10, 2022, conference: Matthew Pottinger, Cortez A. Cooper III, Matsuda Yasuhiro, Sheila Smith, and Jeffrey W. Hornung, *The View of the Taiwan Strait from the U.S.-Japan Alliance*, RAND Corporation, CF-A2070-4, 2023, www.rand.org/t/CFA2070-4.

CHAPTER 2

Four Lessons Ukraine Can Teach the U.S.-Japan Alliance About a Conflict in Taiwan

In the 16 months since Russian leader Vladimir Putin invaded Ukraine, there have been countless analytical pieces written that conclude that his misstep helped revive Western solidarity.[1] There have also been assessments looking at the lessons from the war. Peter Singer, for example, focused on current military thinking and technologies for future wars.[2] Stephen Walt looked at larger strategic lessons for leaders and their publics, such as the ability of leaders to miscalculate or the tendency of states to unite to counter aggression.[3] And Joseph Nye argued the war has reminded us of several lessons, including the importance of nuclear deterrence, the ability to weaponize economic interdependence, and the general unpredictability of war.[4]

Thousands of miles away, in the Indo-Pacific region, the war has become a leading topic of discussion as a much more practical matter. Arguably,

---

1 "How Russia Has Revived NATO," *The Economist*, February 12, 2022.

2 Peter Singer, "One Year In: What Are the Lessons from Ukraine for the Future of War?" *Defense One*, February 22, 2023.

3 Steven Walt, "The Top 5 Lessons from Year One of Ukraine's War," *Foreign Policy*, February 9, 2023.

4 Joseph Nye, Jr., "Eight Lessons from the Ukraine War," *Diplomatic Courier*, June 19, 2022.

nowhere is this attention more piqued than in Taiwan.[5] This is because as mainland China has built up its military and conducted more military operations around Taiwan, President Xi Jinping's rhetoric regarding "reunification" with Taiwan has only gotten stronger.[6] Analysis on what China is learning from the war and how the People's Liberation Army (PLA) may be adapting has offered insight into how Xi may be adjusting his strategy for a potential invasion of Taiwan.[7] At the same time, it has offered experts a chance to examine what Taiwan may be learning to prepare its defenses for a possible conflict.[8] There has even been analysis arguing against what are seen as the wrong lessons for Taiwan.[9]

What could benefit from more discussion is the potential lessons that the U.S.-Japan alliance should draw from Ukraine. Make no mistake, there is much analysis on how Russia's aggression is motivating Japan to do more for its security and strategic thinking. Some prominent names, including the late Prime Minister Abe Shinzō, have argued that Russia's invasion of a non-nuclear Ukraine should have provided momentum for a debate in the

---

5 Michael Schuman, "Is Taiwan Next?" *The Atlantic*, February 24, 2022; Tiejun Zhang, "China Is Not Russia; Taiwan Is Not Ukraine," *The Diplomat*, July 25, 2022; Chris Horton, "The Lessons Taiwan Is Learning from Ukraine," *The Atlantic*, May 7, 2022; Francis Sempa, "The Difference Between Ukraine and Taiwan," *The Diplomat*, January 31, 2022.

6 Hilton Yip, "Taiwan Is Rethinking Defense in Wake of Ukraine Invasion," *Foreign Policy*, February 28, 2022.

7 Joel Wuthnow, "Rightsizing Chinese Military Lessons from Ukraine," *Strategic Forum*, Center for the Study of Chinese Military Affairs, Institute for National Strategic Studies, National Defense University, September 2022; Carole Landry, "The Taiwan Connection," *New York Times*, August 2, 2022.

8 Nathalie Tocci, "Taiwan Has Learned a Lot from the War in Ukraine—It's Time Europe Caught Up," *Politico*, December 20, 2022; Center for Strategic and International Studies, "Ukraine and Taiwan: Parallels and Early Lessons Learned," webpage, March 22, 2022; Marc Santora and Steven Erlanger, "Taiwan and Ukraine: Two Crises, 5,000 Miles Apart, Are Linked in Complex Ways," *New York Times*, August 3, 2022; Laura Kelly, "Invasion Checklists and Survival Academies: How Taiwan Is Preparing for War," *The Hill*, June 8, 2023.

9 Franz-Stefan Gady, "6 Wrong Lessons for Taiwan from the War in Ukraine," *Foreign Policy*, November 2, 2022.

U.S.-Japan alliance on the idea of the allies engaging in "nuclear sharing."[10] Although there was no consensus on this, there is a much broader set of arguments about the effects that the war in Ukraine is having on Japanese strategic thinking. Hikotani Takako, for example, argues that the war has led to profound changes in Japanese society toward the outside world and for Japan's own security, allowing Tokyo to take more supportive positions on Ukraine and play a more constructive role in Japan's own response.[11] Similarly, Nagashima Jun argues the Kishida administration's decision to strengthen its security posture, as symbolized by the December 2022 strategic documents, was motivated, in part, by Russia's attempt to unilaterally change the status quo by force.[12] Others are more prescriptive. Former Ministry of Defense official Tokuchi Hideshi argues that the Russian invasion should impress upon Japan the need not to only focus on the "flashy areas" but to also take a comprehensive look at all issues, including those that do not normally receive much attention, such as logistics.[13]

Examined less is how the alliance is filtering Ukraine's lessons and applying them to its joint strategies and planning, albeit with some notable exceptions. The monthly journal *Gaikō*, for example, included a conversation with three security experts touching on the need to deepen security cooperation with allies and revisit operational planning and the alliance's roles, missions, and capabilities.[14] And Ogi Hirohito argued that, compared with its efforts in Europe, the United States is not ready to provide sufficient

---

10 "The Situation in Ukraine and Japan's Diplomacy and Security" ["ウクライナ情勢と日本の外交、安全保障"], Foreign Press Center Japan, April 22, 2022.

11 Takako Hikotani, "How the Ukraine War Is Changing Japan," *Foreign Affairs*, April 28, 2022.

12 Jun Nagashima, "Japan's Multilateral Cooperation After the Three Security Documents—Strengthening Partnerships with European Countries in New Domains, Advanced Technology, and Supply Chains," Sasakawa Peace Foundation, March 20, 2023.

13 Tokuchi Hideshi, "What to Do About Japan's Defense Capabilities: What to Consider in Formulating a New National Security Strategy" ["日本の防衛力整備をどうするのか—新たな国家安全保障戦略の策定に向けて考えるべきこと"], Nippon.com, September 13, 2022.

14 "Special Feature: Security Strategies Shift" ["特集安保戦略は転換する"], *Gaikō* [外交], Vol. 77, January/February 2023, pp. 14–26.

means of defense against China in a conflict, leaving Japan's self-help efforts and the further improvement of U.S.-Japan interoperability as key to the region's security.[15] And yet, as defense planners in Europe are doing, alliance planners should be studying the weapons, tactics, strategies, and logistics occurring in Ukraine as a means to gain insight into a possible conflict over Taiwan that involves the U.S. and Japanese armed forces. Although acknowledging the risk of drawing lessons from another country's war and applying them to different circumstances, this section considers possible lessons Ukraine could teach U.S.-Japan alliance planners to consider for preparing for a possible regional conflict.

Challenges and Implications

In other venues, the author of these conference proceedings has focused on specific operational questions the alliance should be asking itself to best prepare for a potential conflict.[16] Below, based on insights derived from the RAND-hosted fall 2022 conference, the focus turns instead to broader questions the U.S.-Japan alliance will surely confront should they find themselves facing a conflict in the East China Sea region that involves China attacking Taiwan. Specifically, the examination focuses on four challenges: (1) China's economy being much larger and more integrated with the global economy than Russia's; (2) large-scale displacement and evacuation of civilians and foreign nationals from an island environment; (3) supplying weapons and munitions to fighting forces once conflict commences; and (4) maintaining critical energy supplies to Northeast Asian economies. Learning how the United States and its allies are dealing with these issues in Ukraine could provide useful lessons for the U.S.-Japan alliance when thinking about how

[15] Ogi Hirohito, "The Maximum Impact of the Russia-Ukraine War on Japan" ["ロシアウクライナ戦争が日本に及ぼす最大影響"], *Tōyō Keizai Online* [東洋経済 *Online*], November 7, 2022.

[16] Jeffrey W. Hornung, "Taiwan and Six Potential New Year's Resolutions for the U.S.-Japan Alliance," *War on the Rocks*, January 5, 2022; Jeffrey W. Hornung, "Ukraine Should Provide Japan's Wake-Up Call," *Defense News*, March 24, 2022; Jeffrey W. Hornung, "Six Lessons from Ukraine for Japanese Defense Planners," *War on the Rocks*, June 21, 2023.

best to prepare for a possible war in the East China Sea region. In that spirit, the analysis offers the following four potential implications the allies could be learning regarding these challenges:

1. Any coalition may encounter limits to the effectiveness of creating and maintaining a sanctions regime against China.
2. Current preparation and coordination for a potential noncombatant evacuation operation (NEO) are insufficient.
3. Reliable access to weapons and munitions that are not prepositioned in abundance will be challenging.
4. Stockpiling more energy reserves (where possible) or relying more heavily on domestic renewable energy supplies is needed.

Challenge: China's Economy Is Much Larger and More Integrated with the Global Economy Than Russia's

Implication: Any Coalition May Encounter Limits to the Effectiveness of Creating and Maintaining a Sanctions Regime Against China

Following Russia's invasion of Ukraine, the West's initial response came in the financial realm. Starting on February 24, 2023, the United States and its allies quickly imposed several severe sanctions and associated punitive economic measures on Russia (collectively referred to below as *sanctions* or *sanctions regime*). Subsequent packages of sanctions have resulted in an unparalleled set of measures targeting the key sectors of the Russian economy and Putin and his political allies. Not surprising, key Russian trading partners, such as Brazil, India, China, South Africa, and Turkey, did not impose sanctions. The result was a multilateral sanctions regime with plenty of opportunities for evasion.

These sanctions targeted Russian banks, companies, and markets and more than 1,000 officials who are subject to asset freezes and travel bans.[17] Targeting Russian energy exports has also been a priority. Energy (i.e., oil,

[17] Samuel Petrequin, Raf Casert, and Lorne Cook, "European Union Countries Agree on a New Package of Sanctions Against Russia over the War in Ukraine," Associated Press, June 21, 2023.

gas, coal, and nuclear) is an important part of the Russian economy and an essential source of income for the Russian government. Oil alone provides almost one-half of Russia's budget revenues.[18] One of the harshest punitive measures was removing select Russian banks from the Society for Worldwide Interbank Financial Telecommunication (SWIFT), which executes international transactions between banks. Within days of Russia's invasion, many Russian banks were removed from the system.

Although these sanctions have been widespread and historic in their scope and scale, reaching consensus within a coalition was not always easy. When Russia initially invaded Ukraine, one of the main areas of contention was agreeing on who should receive sanctions, what they would encompass, and how they would be applied. With SWIFT, for example, many European financial institutions were careful to keep Russian connections to the system intact. Germany, for example, was initially reluctant to ban Russia from SWIFT.[19] The motivation for some countries to want to implement the ban in a more selective manner was the concern that a total ban would lead to disruptions to Russia's energy supply to Europe and possibly further increases in energy and food prices.[20] This factor led some European countries to call for exclusions of some Russian banks to the SWIFT ban. Two of the most significant exclusions were Sberbank and Gazprombank because of their leading position in Russian natural gas and oil transactions.[21]

Another area in which there was some challenge in reaching consensus occurred in discussions over sanctions of Russia's energy exports. Russia was the second-largest producer of natural gas globally (16.6 percent of total global natural gas supply in 2020), with the majority of its domestic natural gas production going to Europe to meet about 45 percent of the region's

18 Anna Caprile and Angelos Delivorias, "EU Sanctions on Russia: Overview, Impact, Challenges," European Parliament, March 2023.

19 Hans von der Burchard, "Germany's Olaf Scholz Opposes Inclusion of Swift in Russia Sanctions for Now," *Politico*, February 24, 2022.

20 Alessandro Rebucci, "Swift Sanction on Russia: How It Works and Likely Impacts," *Econofact*, March 4, 2022.

21 Stephen Cecchetti, Kermit L. Schoenholtz, and Richard Berner, "Russian Sanctions: Some Questions and Answers," Centre for Economic Policy Research, March 21, 2022.

import demand.[22] This dependence on Russian energy became a stumbling block in applying some sanctions.[23] Germany, for example, showed reluctance to target Russia's energy sector given its dependence on Russian energy, particularly sanctions meant to target natural gas.[24] Germany was not alone because, in December 2021, approximately one-third (around 2.4 million barrels per day) of Russia's oil was sold to Europe, the largest buyer of Russian oil.[25] Similarly, some countries, such as Hungary, were reluctant to target Russian state nuclear energy company Rosatom, insisting on its importance for Europe's security and environmental goals.[26] The result of these diverging views, based on European dependence on Russian energy, meant that the United States could place more sanctions on different parts of the Russian economy in the first year of the war (2,099) compared with the European Union (1,155).[27] Despite these challenges, the United States and its allies were successful in applying harsh sanctions. The results of these efforts not only send the Kremlin a strong signal of Western resolve and unity but also permanently degrade Russia's military capabilities and suffocate its economy with long-term consequences.[28]

The United States will likely face more difficulties should it try to assemble a similar coalition of economies to apply quick and harsh sanctions on China. Consider first the differences in sizes of the Chinese economy versus the Russian economy prior to the war. In 2021, China's gross domestic product was $17.73 trillion compared with Russia's $1.77 trillion; in other

---

[22] "What's Next for Oil and Gas Prices as Sanctions on Russia Intensify," J.P. Morgan, March 10, 2022.

[23] Gabriel Gavin and Victor Jack, "EU Balks at Adding Russian Gas Pipeline Ban to Sanctions Package," *Politico*, May 16, 2023.

[24] In 2021, for example, Russia supplied more than one-half of Germany's natural gas and one-third of its oil. Melissa Eddy, "Why Germany Can't Just Pull the Plug on Russian Energy," *New York Times*, April 5, 2022.

[25] Caprile and Delivorias, 2023.

[26] Petrequin, Casert, and Cook, 2023.

[27] Statista, "Total Number of List-Based Sanctions Imposed on Russia by Territories and Organizations from February 22, 2022 to February 10, 2023, by Selected Actor," May 12, 2023.

[28] Caprile and Delivorias, 2023.

words, roughly ten times larger.[29] Additionally, Chinese banks had more than 30 times as many assets as Russian banks prior to the war, and cumulative investments into China were more than six times that which went into Russia.[30] These differences mean that China is much more economically integrated with other countries than Russia was, making it much more difficult to punish China without hurting oneself. Potentially problematic is some of China's top trading partners are those states whose participation in sanctions would be critical, such as Japan, South Korea, Germany, and the United Kingdom, not to mention the United States.[31] A further complication is that, unlike Russian oligarchs with large overseas investments, Xi appears to have barred Chinese officials from owning property abroad or stakes in overseas companies, all in the hopes of making China immune to the types of sanctions the West is leveling on Russia.[32]

These facts may not only make it difficult to establish a coalition of states to punish China, they may create means by which to soften Western sanctions. In the case of Ukraine, the West failed to win over many states that share not only ideological ties with Russia, but also economic ties. In the United Nations (UN), for example, in a vote to demand Russia to unconditionally withdraw, 47 countries abstained or missed the vote. Many of these countries have gone on to provide crucial economic support to Russia, helping it evade the bite of sanctions.[33] In a case in which China' importance as a trading partner is much greater, it may be more difficult to get states to sanction China, or sustain those sanctions over long periods. Similarly, if Chinese officials are limited in holding overseas assets, depending on how strictly that policy is enforced, it could cushion China from geopolitical

[29] World Bank, "GDP (Current US$)," webpage, last updated 2021.

[30] Gerard DiPippo, "Deterrence First: Applying Lessons from Sanctions on Russia to China," Center for Strategic and International Studies, May 3, 2022.

[31] World Integrated Trade System (World Bank), "China, Exports and Imports," webpage, last updated 2020.

[32] Chun Han Wong, "China Insists Party Elites Shed Overseas Assets, Eyeing Western Sanctions on Russia," *Wall Street Journal*, May 19, 2022.

[33] Josh Holder, Lauren Leatherby, Anton Troianovski, and Weiyi Cai, "The West Tried to Isolate Russia. It Didn't Work," *New York Times*, February 23, 2023.

risks should the West try to impose sanctions on party officials and family members as a means to push its leadership to back down over Taiwan.

Together, these aspects suggest that there may be limits to relying on sanctions to punish or deter China in a conflict involving Taiwan. Even if a sanctions initiative is led by the world's largest and third-largest economies, other countries may be reluctant to enact sanctions that may substantially hurt their own economies. And China may be making moves to cushion itself from any such actions, making the job of the allies much more difficult. Given these limitations, the allies could make stronger efforts to increase the diversification of trading partners away from China to allow for more options in the economic realm.

Challenge: Large-Scale Displacement and Evacuation of Civilians and Foreign Nationals from an Island Environment

Implication: Current Preparation and Coordination for a Potential NEO Are Insufficient

One of the defining characteristics of the early stages of the Ukraine conflict was the need to rapidly evacuate the civilian population. According to the UN, the war caused the displacement (both internally and externally) of roughly one-third of the country's population of 43 million.[34] Because of the need to retain men who are capable of fighting, the Ukrainian government issued a law preventing men ages 18 to 60 from leaving. As a result of this law, roughly 90 percent of Ukraine's refugees have been women and children.[35] On the day Russia invaded Ukraine, the Ukrainian government closed its airspace to all commercial air travel, leaving ground travel as the only way for civilians to leave or move around the country.[36] In the first month of the conflict, the primary means by which civilians left was via train, with hundreds of thousands of people doing so.[37] Most of these

[34] UN Refugee Agency, "Ukraine Emergency," webpage, undated.

[35] UN Refugee Agency, undated.

[36] Beth Timmins, "Ukraine Airspace Closed to Civilian Flights," BBC, February 24, 2022.

[37] John Bolger, "Ukrainians Fleeing War Fight to Survive on the Rails," *The Nation*, March 8, 2022.

evacuees have gone to neighboring Poland. Because of the rush to evacuate, stampede-like conditions at train stations occurred, requiring Ukrainian police officers to use forceful tactics to maintain control.[38] With train stations crowded, Ukrainians also chose to flee by car or bus, but these options also resulted in crowded roadways. The lines at some border crossings were so crowded that Ukrainians often took days to get through (e.g., 22-mile traffic jam outside the Polish border in late February 2022).[39]

An invasion of Taiwan would likely see a similar pattern of civilians trying to flee the island in the early days of the conflict. Those fleeing will include not just Taiwanese citizens but also foreign nationals residing in Taiwan. As of April 2023, there are approximately 23 million people living in Taiwan.[40] Of those, there are more than 800,000 foreign nationals, which includes 16,768 people from Japan and 11,454 people from the United States.[41] However, unlike Ukraine, where citizens could leave on their own by numerous land options, any evacuation of Taiwan is likely to be more complicated because it is surrounded by water. This factor, in turn, would likely require assisting states to conduct some type of NEO to help Taiwanese and foreign nationals evacuate by sea or air. This effort raises two fundamental areas that the U.S.-Japan alliance needs to consider regardless of whether they are involved in the fighting of the conflict.

First, is the U.S.-Japan alliance prepared to conduct an NEO? The challenge here is twofold: one at the points of embarkation and one at the points of disembarkation. With the former, the allies will need to plan for getting people off Taiwan in what could be rapidly deteriorating security environment. That challenge with this plan, if people assume the western side of Taiwan is susceptible to Chinese attacks, is that the NEO will likely have to be conducted from the eastern side of Taiwan. Problematically, the majority

[38] Bolger, 2022.

[39] Andrew Marshall, "Stuck for Days in Their Cars, Ukrainians Wait to Flee," Reuters, February 28, 2022.

[40] National Statistics (Republic of China), "Total Population," April 23, 2023.

[41] Ministry of the Interior, National Immigration Agency (Taiwan), "Foreign Residents by Nationality, April 2023," May 25, 2023.

of Taiwan's population density is along the island's west coast.[42] Assuming that people will flee away from combat areas to try to evacuate, not only will this plan require a massive movement of people to areas east (a significant problem in and of itself), but it will require an NEO to be conducted from areas where there are fewer airfields and ports and the transportation infrastructure is not as robust. There are three large ports on Taiwan's east coast (Hualien, Suao, and Taitung), and there are challenges to accessing these ports because they are connected by fewer roads and railways (compared with those on the island's west) and are separated from the rest of Taiwan by mountains.[43] The same is true of airports. Taiwan has 16 public airports and 15 private airfields.[44] Of these, only two public airports are in the east (Hualien and Taitung).[45] The same two cities also house two Taiwan air force bases. Collectively, any NEO that the allies choose to conduct will immediately face problems because of the challenges associated with getting people to embarkation points away from combat areas on the western side of the island and then conducting NEOs from ports that are few in number and relatively underdeveloped to handle the large-scale nature of the operations.

Disembarkation efforts could also prove difficult, as the allies would need to work together in an operation involving civilians from not just their own countries but dozens of others. And unlike Ukraine, where multiple countries are engaged in handling Ukrainian evacuees, the onus of the disembarkation operations would likely fall predominately on Japan, given its geographic proximity and Self-Defense Force (SDF) capabilities. Although the allies have some limited experience conducting NEO-focused exercises,

---

[42] Chris Buckley, Pablo Robles, Marco Hernandez, and Amy Chang Chien, "How China Could Choke Taiwan," *New York Times*, August 25, 2022.

[43] Hualien, for example, is the most populated city on the east coast and is connected to the north and south via two major provincial highways and one railway line and one cross-island provincial highway (see Hualien City Office, "About Hualien City," webpage, undated).

[44] Civil Aeronautics Administration (Taiwan), "Private Airfield," January 19, 2019; Civil Aeronautics Administration (Taiwan), "Introduction to Airports," December 28, 2022.

[45] Maybe three airports, if Taipei Songshan Airport is included in the count.

they have not exercised for the sudden influx of tens of thousands of undocumented people at Japan's airports and sea ports.[46] On the most basic level, it is unclear whether the allies have agreed on where the disembarkation sites in Japan would be. Additionally, despite years of exercising together, it is unclear whether they have coordinated their understandings on their roles in an NEO. For example, if active combat is occurring in and around Taiwan, would the United States be tasked with helping at embarkation sites and Japan with receiving those civilians at disembarkation sites? Finally, there are expected to be difficulties with how Japan can process the sudden arrival of tens of thousands of foreigners. One assessment of NEOs argues that caring for evacuees on their arrival is the most urgent task. This evacuation effort would include such basics as providing food, water, and shelter; providing access to chargers for phones; having formula accessible for babies; and, most importantly, helping evacuees onward to someplace beyond the disembarkation facility.[47] Medical assistance is also critical because many of these evacuees may be injured physically or mentally. There is also expected to be an issue of evacuees not having the proper identification or finances to allow them to freely move throughout Japan and onward to other destinations. At a time that the SDF may be confronted with engaging in combat for the first time in its existence, it may simultaneously have to manage a historically large NEO in multiple points in the country, all while ensuring that domestic order and peace are maintained.

Second, assuming that the SDF is prepared, does it have the training and capabilities to conduct what could amount to history's largest NEO? Even if readers assume the United States takes the lead on getting people off of Taiwan at embarkation points while Japan takes the lead on operations in Japan at disembarkation points as well as rear area support of U.S. forces operating in theater, to date Japan's SDF has never conducted an NEO. When Afghanistan's Ashraf Ghani regime collapsed in August 2021, Tokyo wanted to evacuate around 500 of its own citizens and local embassy support staff. That effort was largely seen as a failure, however, because the

46 John Severns, "U.S. Forces Japan Participates in Annual Non-Combatant Evacuation Operation Exercise," U.S. Indo-Pacific Command, June 16, 2017.

47 Chris Field, "Non-Combatant Evacuation Operations: Six Ideas from August 2021," *The Cove*, October 2, 2022.

government dispatched four aircraft but could only evacuate one Japanese woman and 14 Afghans.[48] The largest NEO that the United States ever performed was Operation Allies Refuge during the same situation, when the U.S. military safely evacuated 124,334 people, including 6,000 Americans, over the course of 17 days.[49] These vastly different experiences belie the fact that any NEO involving Taiwan would be dramatically different from both Afghanistan and Ukraine. To start, there is no established presence of large numbers of U.S. military assets in Taiwan like there was in Afghanistan. Additionally, unlike Afghanistan, where violence was being perpetuated by Taliban insurgents, any Taiwan NEO could very well be in a contested environment involving a highly organized PLA making any NEO difficult for U.S. and Japanese forces. Finally, the NEO in Afghanistan was categorized as easy in that the target was limited to U.S. citizens and to Afghans who had served as interpreters, drivers, and assistants to U.S. forces and diplomats. A Taiwan NEO could involve up to the full 800,000 foreign residents living in Taiwan and tens of thousands of Taiwanese seeking to flee. The sheer numbers of civilians involved in the NEO would put enormous stress on existing U.S. and Japanese lift capabilities, none of which are in Taiwan.

Collectively, all this suggests that, unlike the situation in Ukraine, where civilians were able to evacuate the country largely by their own means, evacuees from Taiwan will face much more difficulty fleeing from the war zone. Without the option of fleeing by train or car, anyone wishing to leave Taiwan will have to depend on such states as the United States and Japan in both helping them escape and receiving them. The sheer number and scope of operations are likely to put enormous stress on the allies in ways not being witnessed in Europe from the war in Ukraine. Collectively, these factors highlight the need for the alliance to make concerted peacetime preparations and coordination for a potential NEO.

---

[48] Kuniichi Tanida, "Examining Japan's Afghanistan Evacuation Operations," Nippon.com, December 9, 2021.

[49] Kristen Duncan, "Air Force Rescue Personnel Support NEO Weeks Before the Fall of Kabul," U.S. Air Force, October 21, 2021; James Kitfield, "Remembering the Largest Non-Combatant Evacuation Operation in US History," *Air & Space Forces Magazine*, August 29, 2022.

Challenge: Supplying Weapons and Munitions to Fighting Forces Once Conflict Commences

Implication: Reliable Access to Weapons and Munitions That Are not Prepositioned in Abundance Will Be Challenging

One of the more noteworthy aspects of Ukraine's defense has been its interception of Russian missiles and drones. According to one report, Ukraine has intercepted these capabilities via S-300/SA-10 and Buk-M1/SA-11 surface-to-air missile systems, all leftover systems from stockpiles from the Soviet Union era, with about a one-to-one success rate of 80 percent.[50] Ukraine has also relied on various types of other missiles for air defenses from Western sources, such as the IRIS-T, NASAM, and Patriot systems, among others.[51] It is possible that Ukraine's success against these missiles has been because Russia has been firing fairly small salvos of missiles that have been largely subsonic in nature, mainly short-and medium-range ballistic weapons, cruise missiles, surface-to-air missiles, and sea-launched missiles.[52] However, Russia has used its Kinzhal hypersonic missiles, which have proven much more difficult to intercept and requiring Ukraine to fire multiple interceptor missiles.[53]

Relentless bombardments from Russia have made clear the importance of keeping Ukraine's munition stockpiles full. Russia started the war with a huge stockpile, which some argue gave it a battlefield advantage; but the nature of the protracted conflict has meant that those stockpiles have been drawn down.[54] The same with Ukraine: According to one estimate, the average use of Ukrainian interceptor missiles alone is about 157 mis-

---

[50] Mark F. Cancian, "Will Russia Control the Skies over Ukraine?" Center for Strategic and International Studies, April 25, 2023.

[51] Kristyna Foltynova, "Protecting the Skies: How Does Ukraine Defend Against Russian Missiles?" *Radio Free Europe Radio Liberty*, December 24, 2022.

[52] Alex Horton, "The Russian Weaponry Being Used to Attack Ukraine," *Washington Post*, February 24, 2022.

[53] Natasha Bertrand and Oren Liebermann, "Russia Tried to Destroy US-Made Patriot System in Ukraine, Officials Say," CNN, May 12, 2023.

[54] Matthew Luxmoore, "Russia Exploits Artillery Advantage as Ukraine Braces for Attacks on More Eastern Cities," *Wall Street Journal*, June 11, 2022.

siles per month.[55] The West has sought to assist Ukraine through the shipment of weapons and munitions.[56] As of March 2023, the United States provided more than $30 billion worth of such assistance.[57] It has shipped 8,500-plus Javelin anti-tank missiles, 32,000-plus other anti-tank missiles, at least 561,000 155-mm artillery shells, 1,400-plus Stinger missiles, an unspecified number of multiple-launch rocket system missiles, and a host of hardware systems (e.g., the High-Mobility Artillery Rocket System, howitzers, counter-artillery radar, and unmanned aerial systems).[58] Although specific routes regarding the delivery of such capabilities are not public, because of Russia's ability to fly throughout Ukrainian airspace, the vast majority of weapons and munitions come via railways and roads.[59] Most of this aid comes into Ukraine via Poland, which itself arrives via aircraft from the United States and other NATO allies.[60] Aid has also been delivered via routes from Slovakia and Romania. As the war dragged on, the United States even began using maritime shipping to deliver larger bulk quantities of weapons.[61] As one snapshot in time of how this support has been delivered, a January 2023 release by the U.S. Transportation Command of U.S. deliveries of munition and support to "allies and partners in Europe" consisted of 1,280 flights, 75 vessels, 143 trains, and more than 8,177 trucks.[62] The United States' efforts to supply Ukraine have been historic. Its ability

---

[55] Cancian, 2023.

[56] Brett Forrest and Jared Malsin, "Ukraine Leans on Armed Turkish Drones, Western Missiles to Thwart Russian Invasion," *Wall Street Journal*, March 3, 2022.

[57] Jim Garamone, "U.S. Sends Ukraine $400 Million in Military Equipment," U.S. Department of Defense, March 3, 2023.

[58] Mark Cancian, "Is the United States Running out of Weapons to Send to Ukraine?" Center for Strategic and International Studies, September 16, 2022.

[59] Vincent E. Castillo, "How Weapons Get to Ukraine and What's Needed to Protect Vulnerable Supply Chains," *The Conversation*, March 16, 2022.

[60] Rob Mudge, "How Are the West's Weapons Getting to Ukraine?" *DW*, March 1, 2022; "How the U.S. Is Getting Weapons to Ukraine," NPR, May 6, 2022.

[61] Dan Lamothe, "Pentagon Expands Use of Seas to Send Weapons to Ukraine," *Washington Post*, August 27, 2022.

[62] U.S. Transportation Command, "Support to Allies and Partners in Europe," undated.

to move millions of pounds of material has been the biggest operation since the Berlin airlift in the late 1940s.[63]

A war anywhere in the East China Sea area will pose logistical challenges more difficult than seen in Ukraine. Whether it be rearming the Taiwan military or even resupplying U.S. troops in Japan or the SDF on any of its outlying islands, the maritime nature of the region makes delivery of any weapons, munitions, or supplies wholly reliant on ships or airplanes. Although this aspect has proven useful for getting munitions into Poland for onward movement, those flights have not come under attack. The situation is likely to be very different in an East China Sea conflict, making resupply efforts extremely difficult.

Consider first any attempts to resupply Taiwan. Given the challenges associated with limited airfields and ports on the eastern side of Taiwan (outlined earlier in this document), any resupply efforts are going to be vulnerable to PLA strikes, particularly because air superiority over Taiwan may be difficult to secure. This means the PLA may be able to intercept any incoming shipments with airstrikes or missile strikes, leaving Taiwan largely to fight the war with its own stockpiles for long periods of time. Resupplying U.S. forces in Japan or the SDF does not face the same challenges that a resupply of Taiwan does, given that it could face a similar situation as Poland, where resupply flights can be brought into more ports of entry away from active combat areas. Nevertheless, resupplying U.S. forces or the SDF during a regional contingency is not without challenge. Like Taiwan, the entire Japanese archipelago is within range of Chinese missiles.[64] Beijing's focus on developing anti-access/area denial capabilities over the past decade has meant that its arsenal of ballistic and cruise missiles can target U.S. and Japanese targets—including ships and planes—anywhere in Japan. Although Japan has a two-tier ballistic missile defense system and a nationwide air and missile defense capability, these are not perfect. This is particularly the case for ships and planes that may be heading to Japan, far from these territorial defenses. And as China begins to employ hyper-

63 "How the U.S. Is Getting Weapons to Ukraine," 2022.

64 Missile Threat, "Missiles of China," CSIS Missile Defense Project, last updated April 12, 2021.

sonic weapons that have increased speed and maneuverability, this task will become more difficult, even for those ships and planes in and around Japan.

Together, the maritime nature of a conflict in the East China Sea, combined with China's expansive arsenal of missiles that put the entire region at risk, suggests that the allies will confront exponentially more difficulties in resupplying forces with critical weapons and munitions than the United States and NATO are experiencing with their efforts to Ukraine. Although delivering these goods to some parts of Japan may be similar to what the allies are facing in Poland today, the potential for China to launch attacks against U.S. forces or ports of entry anywhere in the entire Japanese archipelago means that, while areas in Taiwan and Japan's southwest are likely to face extremely acute challenges, no place in Japan will be in sanctuary. The likely result is suspended, or continuously unpredictable, resupply efforts once a conflict begins. This, in turn, will disrupt operations, as defense equipment could run out of critical munitions because of the difficulty of resupplying. This suggests the need for the allies to ensure that the weapons and munitions they will need in a conflict are prepositioned in abundance.

Challenge: Maintaining Critical Energy Supplies to Northeast Asian Economies

Implication: Stockpiling More Energy Reserves (Where Possible) or Relying More Heavily on Domestic Renewable Energy Supplies Is Needed

One of the immediate concerns that followed Russia's invasion was the impact on energy supplies, both Ukrainian exports and imports. Ukraine is unique because it is both a top energy consumer and producer in Europe.[65] At the start of 2022, prior to the invasion, Ukraine had one of the most developed energy sectors in Europe, with nearly 65 percent of its total energy demand covered by domestic production.[66] This high self-sufficiency is due to its nuclear energy production but also its domestic thermal and combined heating and power plants. Nuclear energy, comprising the largest

[65] U.S. Energy Information Administration, "Ukraine," August 2021.

[66] International Energy Agency, *Ukraine Energy Profile*, April 2020.

amount, represented 55.5 percent of electricity production.[67] This includes the Zaporizhzhia nuclear power plant, one of Ukraine's four nuclear power plants and Europe's largest. Prior to the war, this reactor accounted for 43 percent of Ukraine's total nuclear power and 25 percent of the country's total energy production.[68] Because of Russian forces occupying the plant, operations at the plant have been suspended, and other nuclear power plants have been attacked. The second-largest portion of Ukraine's energy is derived from thermal plants. Prior to the invasion, there were 12 plants operating in Ukraine (using coal as the primary fuel), accounting for 23.8 percent of Ukraine's electricity production.[69] Since the start of the war, Russian forces have occupied three of these plants and damaged (or destroyed) all of them to some degree, resulting in a 78 percent drop in the country's thermal power capacities.[70] The smallest portion of domestic production came from combined heating and power plants, which provided 5.5 percent of electricity production prior to the invasion.[71] Because Russian forces have occupied roughly 8 percent of these plants and have damaged or destroyed at least 48 percent of them, the energy production of these plants has also dropped.[72] For the remainder, Ukraine relied on imports, with reports indicating that it relied on foreign imports for roughly 35 percent of its energy needs.[73] This consists of 83 percent of its oil, 33 percent of its natural gas, and 50 percent of its coal.[74] Of these suppliers, Ukraine's biggest partners for coal and petroleum were Russia, Belarus, Germany, Azerbaijan, and Kazakhstan.[75]

---

[67] Cooperation for Restoring the Ukrainian Energy Infrastructure Project, *Ukrainian Energy Sector Evaluation and Damage Assessment–IX*, International Energy Charter, April 24, 2023.

[68] Cooperation for Restoring the Ukrainian Energy Infrastructure Project, 2023

[69] Cooperation for Restoring the Ukrainian Energy Infrastructure Project, 2023.

[70] Cooperation for Restoring the Ukrainian Energy Infrastructure Project, 2023.

[71] Cooperation for Restoring the Ukrainian Energy Infrastructure Project, 2023.

[72] Cooperation for Restoring the Ukrainian Energy Infrastructure Project, 2023.

[73] U.S. Energy Information Administration, 2021.

[74] International Energy Agency, April 2020.

[75] U.S. Energy Information Administration, 2021.

Russia's invasion has had significant negative consequences for Ukraine's energy sector. Much of this has been felt through the rapid decline in energy production, as noted above. In 2022, the production capacity of Ukrainian power plants decreased from 36.0 gigawatts to 13.9 gigawatts.[76] But Ukraine has also confronted this in other areas. For example, Russia has taken control of Ukrainian mineral deposits, resulting in Ukraine losing 63 percent of coal deposits, 42 percent of metal deposits, 20 percent of natural gas deposits, and 11 percent of oil deposits.[77] The combined effect has meant not just fewer energy supplies for Ukrainians but fewer energy exports abroad. Additionally, the United Nations Development Programme and World Bank estimate that the cost of direct damages to the Ukrainian energy sector is above $10 billion, and 12 million people have suffered from significant energy disruptions.[78] Costs for damaged nuclear power plants alone, for example, are roughly $800 million, while costs for thermal plants are approximately $160 million.[79] One estimate of the cost for complete recovery of Ukraine's energy sector is $47 billion.[80]

Ukraine has mitigated the effects of the loss of its energy supplies through a combination of measures. Central to this effort has been international aid, use of generators, decreased consumption of energy by civilians, a nationwide ban on fuel exports, and efficient repairs to energy infrastructure.[81] Diversification of its supplies away from Russia has also helped. For example, prior to the war, Russia supplied the majority of Ukraine's coal (60 percent). However, after terminating that supply in February 2022, Rus-

[76] United Nations Development Programme and World Bank, *Ukraine Energy Damage Assessment: Executive Summary*, March 2023.

[77] Cooperation for Restoring the Ukrainian Energy Infrastructure Project, 2023.

[78] United Nations Development Programme and World Bank, 2023.

[79] Cooperation for Restoring the Ukrainian Energy Infrastructure Project, 2023; United Nations Development Programme and World Bank, 2023.

[80] Cooperation for Restoring the Ukrainian Energy Infrastructure Project, 2023.

[81] Cooperation for Restoring the Ukrainian Energy Infrastructure Project, 2023; United Nations Development Programme and World Bank, 2023.

sian coal imports in Ukraine dropped to 39 percent as Ukraine pivoted to imports from the United States, Australia, Columbia, and Kazakhstan.[82]

Should a similar conflict erupt over Taiwan, the challenges for such states as the United States and Japan to ensure reliable energy supplies for the island will be much more difficult. According to Taiwan statistics, in 2021, oil, coal, and natural gas made up 43.39 percent, 30.78 percent, and 18.11 percent of Taiwan's total primary energy consumption, respectively, while the remainder was mostly nuclear (5.59 percent) and smaller amounts of various renewable energy sources.[83] As an island, Taiwan imports 97.73 percent of its energy needs.[84] Its demand for natural gas, for example, is met almost completely by imports (99 percent).[85] This is not limited to one commodity or geographic location, because it imports its oil, coal, and natural gas from locations as far as the Middle East and the United States and as close as Indonesia and Australia.[86] Cognizant of its vulnerability to imports, Taiwan maintains energy reserves, but not in large amounts. Its coal reserves, for example, only amounted to 1.1 million tons in 2016, which is less than one year of coal consumption.[87] Its oil reserves are even less, at only 146 days.[88] Because of its heavy dependence on imports, if the PLA imposed a naval blockade, Taiwan would face a situation unlike Ukraine in that it would be extremely difficult to import the necessary energy sources into the island, thereby precipitating the rapid onset of an energy crisis.

---

82 "Ukraine's Coal Imports Up 18% in Q1'2021," *The Coal Hub*, undated; "Ukraine's Coal Imports Down 67% in Jan-Aug 2022," *The Coal Hub*, undated.

83 Bureau of Energy, "Energy Supply in 2021," Ministry of Economic Affairs (Taiwan), July 21, 2022a.

84 Bureau of Energy, 2022a.

85 Bureau of Energy, "Stable Supply of Natural Gas," Ministry of Economic Affairs (Taiwan), November 7, 2022b.

86 U.S. Energy Information Administration, "Taiwan," December 2016.

87 Worldometer, "Taiwan Coal," webpage, undated.

88 Lisa Wang, "Energy Supplies Sufficient, Ministry Says," *Taipei Times*, August 4, 2022.

A conflict over Taiwan would also affect Japan. In fiscal year (FY) 2019, Japan's dependency on fossil fuels stood at 84.8 percent.[89] Oil alone accounts for about 40 percent of Japan's primary energy supply.[90] Importantly, Japan relies heavily on liquefied natural gas (LNG), which accounts for about 24 percent of Japan's total energy mix and for 36 percent of Japan's electricity production.[91] Although it once operated 54 nuclear reactors, the 2011 disaster at Japan's Fukushima power plant led to societal and political pressure to close most of the country's remaining plants. Today, power generated by nuclear plants stands at about 3 percent of Japan's total energy mix (six reactors in operation).[92] Problematically, Japan does not have these resources domestically. Compared with other Organisation for Economic Co-operation and Development countries, Japan has a low energy self-sufficiency ratio (12.1 percent in FY 2019).[93] Before the 2011 triple disasters that resulted in shuttering most of Japan's nuclear facilities, this ratio stood at 20.2 percent (FY 2010), and at one point it reached a low of 6.3 percent (FY 2014).[94]

Because of this low self-sufficiency ratio, Japan depends largely on imported fossil fuels, such as oil, coal, and LNG. In 2019, for example, Japan imported so much fossil fuel that it was the world's largest importer of LNG, third-largest importer of coal, and fourth-largest importer of oil.[95] Because it is an archipelago, these imports arrive in Japan via ship. Data from FY 2021 show that Japan depends on the Middle East for about 90 percent of its crude oil requirements, while it looks to the rest of Asia and Oceania for the majority of its LNG and coal imports.[96] A conflict over Taiwan endan-

[89] METI, "2021—Understanding the Current Energy Situation in Japan (Part 1)," August 12, 2022.

[90] U.S. Energy Information Administration, "Japan," November 2, 2020.

[91] Rocky Swift and Yuka Obayashi, "Explainer: Why Japan's Power Sector Depends So Much on LNG," Reuters, March 9, 2022.

[92] Swift and Obayashi, 2022.

[93] METI, 2022.

[94] METI, 2022.

[95] U.S. Energy Information Administration, 2020.

[96] METI, August 12, 2022.

gers these imports because a war would threaten the stable supply of energy flows that have to transit the South China Sea or areas of the Pacific Ocean east of Taiwan. Cognizant of this fact, the government maintains a robust oil reserve of approximately 480 million barrels, or 240 days' worth, in national and private stockpiles (as of December 2021) but only two to three weeks of LNG reserves because it does not have underground storage facilities.[97] Unlike Taiwan, however, Japan's 386 million tons of coal reserves means it has roughly two years' worth in reserve.[98]

Collectively, this suggests that, although Japan is in a slightly better position than Taiwan to endure disruptions to its energy imports, neither Japan nor Taiwan can sustain routine energy usage throughout a protracted conflict without encountering disruptions. Because of their vulnerabilities to energy imports, any conflict in Northeast Asia will prove damaging to their energy consumption, resulting in much more immediate energy crises than Ukraine has experienced to date. Although ensuring more diversified energy suppliers could potentially assist these economies, stockpiling more energy reserves (where possible) or relying more heavily on domestic renewable energy supplies may be their best bet to weather some of the expected difficulties that are expected to arise.

Ways Ahead

As speakers in both sessions of the RAND-hosted fall 2022 conference pointed out, any attack by China on Taiwan will likely involve the U.S.-Japan alliance in several capacities. Regardless of what roles and missions are decided in the military domain, a quick and unified effort vis-à-vis this aggression will be required to maintain the peace and stability of the region and ensure Japan's defense. The four areas examined above highlighted some of the important areas that the allies will necessarily confront if hostilities erupt. To better prepare the allies to respond to this circumstance, the following are a few specific ideas drawn from the broader lessons outlined above that the allies can consider in peacetime.

[97] Swift and Obayashi, 2022.

[98] Worldometer, "Japan Coal," webpage, undated.

Sanctions regime: Should the U.S.-Japan alliance agree that stopping Chinese aggression is in their vested interest, a coordinated international response to punish Beijing economically will likely be included in their efforts. Understanding that cutting off Chinese banks from SWIFT and putting sanctions on Chinese goods and secondary sanctions on countries willing to trade with China may be difficult, the allies should focus on areas that could harm China's war effort, such as applying export controls on dual-use technology and industrial components and, where possible, energy exports. In addition, although leadership assets may not be overseas, the allies could work with like-minded countries to ban Chinese planes from their airspace and ships from their ports to force Chinese citizens to remain in China. Arguably, the most difficult of these efforts would be to work with private corporations to end their business relationships with China or withhold Western products from the Chinese markets. The objective of all these efforts should be to weaken China's economic base and curtail its ability to wage war, either through activities that provide income or by making it difficult to obtain access to critical military technologies and components. Additionally, efforts at isolating Chinese travel and investments are meant to target political and economic elites to undermine their support for the Chinese Communist Party. Because of China's integration with the world economy, none of these efforts are likely to be easy, and getting countries to join these efforts could be difficult. Therefore, the allies should concurrently focus their efforts on finding ways to help Taiwan with economic aid packages.

Weapons and munitions: Japan's defense plans show a renewed effort toward stockpiling munitions. Because there will be no public ability to check government efforts, it is up to the government of Japan to ensure follow-through on maintaining sufficient stockpiles of these precision-guided munitions to enable it to maintain an active defense. Because newer, modern munitions will necessitate updated storage facilities, Japan should also ensure that these depots are located where the allies are expected to actively use them in a conflict. This plan should be augmented by robust air and sealift capabilities to ensure replenishment throughout the archipelago. Additionally, the allies could work to establish sufficient production lines that both allies can draw on to ensure that they are not overburdening single suppliers of critical weapons. Finally, the allies should make a concerted effort to strengthen their passive defenses around bases and facilities (i.e., hardened munition depots, hardened fuel and communication lines, hardened aircraft shelters, decoys) to ensure better protection for these prepositioned munitions and weapons. Ensuring that Japan maintains its robust air and missile defenses will also support any resupply efforts expected to enter into Japan.

Civilian displacement: Understanding that Japan will be the likely destination for bringing evacuees from Taiwan, the allies should first identify likely civilian airports and sea ports that can handle large influxes of people. Once those are identified, the allies should start to stockpile critical resources and relief items. Therefore, this type of preparation should be included in alliance discussions and planning. Having U.S. and Japanese forces exercise for NEOs also should be a routine part of their annual training schedules. Additionally, the allies should ensure not only that Japan has an NEO doctrine, but that the United States and Japan have a joint doctrine on this issue so that they can promote interoperability with their doctrines, terminologies, and rules of engagement to better clarify their expected roles and missions.

Energy supplies: Because of the difficulty of ensuring stable energy flows into Japan during a conflict, it is important for Japan to establish an optimal combination of power sources that can provide a stable energy supply even when imports are disrupted. This energy mix should continue to include some level of nuclear energy while maximizing the use of renewable energy. Additionally, the allies should focus on ways that the United States can supplement the LNG and oil needs of Japan and Taiwan (and the broader region) should other exports shrink.[99] This is particularly attractive given that the United States is the world's largest LNG exporter. That said, because LNG and oil rely on maritime trade, they are under the same vulnerabilities as other exporters; this puts a premium of maximizing domestic energy sources in peacetime.

[99] In 2022, U.S. companies provided 50 percent of Europe's LNG supplies and 12 percent of its oil (see Ben LeFebre, "How American Energy Helped Europe Best Putin," *Politico*, February 23, 2023).

Conclusion

Keeping with the theme of the two RAND-hosted conferences and the possible lessons from the war in Ukraine to inform the U.S.-Japan alliance, this section examined four broad challenges that the allies would surely confront in a conflict in the East China Sea. Collectively, the section argued that the allies could expect greater difficulties than in Ukraine in the areas of creating and maintaining a sanctions regime, handling the displacement and evacuation of civilians, supplying weapons and munitions to forces fighting in theater, and maintaining energy supplies. If the Ukraine war has taught nations anything, it is the importance of having allies and partners work together toward a common purpose. Should a war breakout in Northeast Asia, the current war in Ukraine offers valuable lessons for the United States and Japan in their efforts.

Abbreviations

FY	fiscal year
LNG	liquefied natural gas
NATO	North Atlantic Treaty Organization
NEO	noncombatant evacuation operation
PLA	People's Liberation Army
SDF	Self-Defense Forces
SWIFT	Society for Worldwide Interbank Financial Telecommunication

References

Bertrand, Natasha, and Oren Liebermann, “Russia Tried to Destroy US-Made Patriot System in Ukraine, Officials Say,” CNN, May 12, 2023.

Bolger, John, “Ukrainians Fleeing War Fight to Survive on the Rails,” *The Nation*, March 8, 2022.

Buckley, Chris, Pablo Robles, Marco Hernandez and Amy Chang Chien, “How China Could Choke Taiwan,” *New York Times*, August 25, 2022.

Burchard, Hans von der, “Germany’s Olaf Scholz Opposes Inclusion of Swift in Russia Sanctions for Now,” *Politico*, February 24, 2022.

Bureau of Energy, “Energy Supply in 2021,” Ministry of Economic Affairs (Taiwan), July 21, 2022a.

Bureau of Energy, “Stable Supply of Natural Gas,” Ministry of Economic Affairs (Taiwan), November 7, 2022b.

Cancian, Mark, “Is the United States Running Out of Weapons to Send to Ukraine?” Center for Strategic and International Studies, September 16, 2022.

Cancian, Mark, “Will Russia Control the Skies over Ukraine?” Center for Strategic and International Studies, April 25, 2023.

Caprile, Anna, and Angelos Delivorias, “EU Sanctions on Russia: Overview, Impact, Challenges,” European Parliament, March 2023.

Castillo, Vincent, “How Weapons Get to Ukraine and What’s Needed to Protect Vulnerable Supply Chains,” *The Conversation*, March 16, 2022.

Cecchetti, Stephen, Kermit L. Schoenholtz, and Richard Berner, “Russian Sanctions: Some Questions and Answers,” Centre for Economic Policy Research, March 21, 2022.

Center for Strategic and International Studies, “Ukraine and Taiwan: Parallels and Early Lessons Learned,” webpage, March 22, 2022.

Civil Aeronautics Administration (Taiwan), “Private Airfield,” webpage, last updated January 19, 2019. As of June 26, 2023: https://www.caa.gov.tw/article.aspx?a=227&lang=2

Civil Aeronautics Administration (Taiwan), “Introduction to Airports,” webpage, last updated December 28, 2022. As of June 26, 2023: https://www.caa.gov.tw/Article.aspx?a=532&lang=2

Cooperation for Restoring the Ukrainian Energy Infrastructure Project, *Ukrainian Energy Sector Evaluation and Damage Assessment–IX*, International Energy Charter, April 24, 2023.

DiPippo, Gerard, "Deterrence First: Applying Lessons from Sanctions on Russia to China," Center for Strategic and International Studies, May 3, 2022.

Duncan, Kristen, "Air Force Rescue Personnel Support NEO Weeks Before the Fall of Kabul," U.S. Air Force, October 21, 2021.

Eddy, Melissa, "Why Germany Can't Just Pull the Plug on Russian Energy," *New York Times*, April 5, 2022.

Field, Chris, "Non-Combatant Evacuation Operations: Six Ideas from August 2021," *The Cove*, October 2, 2022.

Foltynova, Kristyna, "Protecting the Skies: How Does Ukraine Defend Against Russian Missiles?" *Radio Free Europe/Radio Liberty*, December 24, 2022.

Forrest, Brett and Jared Malsin, "Ukraine Leans on Armed Turkish Drones, Western Missiles to Thwart Russian Invasion," *Wall Street Journal*, March 3, 2022.

Gady, Franz-Stefan, "6 Wrong Lessons for Taiwan from the War in Ukraine," *Foreign Policy*, November 2, 2022.

Garamone, Jim, "U.S. Sends Ukraine $400 Million in Military Equipment," U.S. Department of Defense, March 3, 2023.

Gavin, Gabriel, and Victor Jack, "EU Balks at Adding Russian Gas Pipeline Ban to Sanctions Package," *Politico*, May 16, 2023.

Hikotani, Takako, "How the Ukraine War Is Changing Japan," *Foreign Affairs*, April 28, 2022.

Holder, Josh, Lauren Leatherby, Anton Troianovski, and Weiyi Cai, "The West Tried to Isolate Russia. It Didn't Work," *New York Times*, February 23, 2023.

Hornung, Jeffrey W., "Taiwan and Six Potential New Year's Resolutions for the U.S.-Japan Alliance," *War on the Rocks*, January 5, 2022a.

Hornung, Jeffrey W., "Ukraine Should Provide Japan's Wake-Up Call," *Defense News*, March 24, 2022b.

Hornung, Jeffrey W., "Six Lessons from Ukraine for Japanese Defense Planners," *War on the Rocks*, June 21, 2023.

Horton, Alex, "The Russian Weaponry Being Used to Attack Ukraine," *Washington Post*, February 24, 2022.

Horton, Chris, "The Lessons Taiwan Is Learning from Ukraine," *The Atlantic*, May 7, 2022.

"How Russia Has Revived NATO," *The Economist*, February 12, 2022.

"How the U.S. Is Getting Weapons to Ukraine," NPR, May 6, 2022.

Hualien City Office, "About Hualien City," webpage, undated. As of June 21, 2023:
https://www.hualien.gov.tw/content_edit.php?menu=2620&typeid=2620

International Energy Agency, *Ukraine Energy Profile*, April 2020.

Kelly, Laura, "Invasion Checklists and Survival Academies: How Taiwan Is Preparing for War," *The Hill*, June 8, 2023.

Kitfield, James, "Remembering the Largest Non-Combatant Evacuation Operation in US History," *Air & Space Forces Magazine*, August 29, 2022.

Lamothe, Dan, "Pentagon Expands Use of Seas to Send Weapons to Ukraine," *Washington Post*, August 27, 2022.

Landry, Carole, "The Taiwan Connection," *New York Times*, August 2, 2022.

LeFebre, Ben, "How American Energy Helped Europe Best Putin," *Politico*, February 23, 2023.

Luxmoore, Matthew, "Russia Exploits Artillery Advantage as Ukraine Braces for Attacks on More Eastern Cities," *Wall Street Journal*, June 11, 2022.

Marshall, Andrew, "Stuck for Days in Their Cars, Ukrainians Wait to Flee," Reuters, February 28, 2022.

METI, "2021—Understanding the Current Energy Situation in Japan (Part 1)," webpage, August 12, 2022. As of June 22, 2023:
https://www.enecho.meti.go.jp/en/category/special/article/detail_171.html#:~:text=Japan%20depends%20on%20the%20Middle,for%20Japan%20will%20be%20jeopardized

Ministry of the Interior, National Immigration Agency (Taiwan), "Foreign Residents by Nationality, April 2023," May 25, 2023.

Missile Threat, "Missiles of China," CSIS Missile Defense Project, webpage, last updated April 12, 2021. As of June 21, 2023:
https://missilethreat.csis.org/country/china/

Mudge, Rob, "How Are the West's Weapons Getting to Ukraine?" *DW*, March 1, 2022.

Nagashima, Jun, "Japan's Multilateral Cooperation After the Three Security Documents—Strengthening Partnerships with European Countries in New Domains, Advanced Technology, and Supply Chains," Sasakawa Peace Foundation, March 20, 2023.

National Statistics (Republic of China), "Total Population," webpage, April 23, 2023. As of June 19, 2023:
https://eng.stat.gov.tw/Point.aspx?sid=t.9&n=4208&sms=11713

Nye, Joseph, Jr., "Eight Lessons from the Ukraine War," *Diplomatic Courier*, June 19, 2022

Ogi Hirohito, "The Maximum Impact of the Russia-Ukraine War on Japan" ["ロシアウクライナ戦争が日本に及ぼす最大影響"], *Tōyō Keizai Online* [東洋経済], November 7, 2022.

Petrequin, Samuel, Raf Casert, and Lorne Cook, "European Union Countries Agree on a New Package of Sanctions Against Russia over the War in Ukraine," Associated Press, June 21, 2023.

Rebucci, Alessandro, "Swift Sanction on Russia: How It Works and Likely Impacts," *Econofact*, March 4, 2022.

Santora, Marc, and Steven Erlanger, "Taiwan and Ukraine: Two Crises, 5,000 Miles Apart, Are Linked in Complex Ways," *New York Times*, August 3, 2022.

Schuman, Michael, "Is Taiwan Next?" *The Atlantic*, February 24, 2022.

Sempa, Francis, "The Difference Between Ukraine and Taiwan," *The Diplomat*, January 31, 2022.

Severns, John, "U.S. Forces Japan Participates in Annual Non-Combatant Evacuation Operation Exercise," U.S. Indo-Pacific Command, June 16, 2017.

Singer, Peter, "One Year In: What Are the Lessons from Ukraine for the Future of War?" *Defense One*, February 22, 2023.

"The Situation in Ukraine and Japan's Diplomacy and Security" ["ウクライナ情勢と日本の外交、安全保障"], Foreign Press Center Japan, April 22, 2022.

"Special Feature: Security Strategies Shift" ["特集安保戦略は転換する"], *Gaikō* [外交], Vol. 77, January/February 2023.

Statista, "Total Number of List-Based Sanctions Imposed on Russia by Territories and Organizations from February 22, 2022 to February 10, 2023, by Selected Actor," webpage, February 2023. As of June 23, 2023: https://www.statista.com/statistics/1294752/sanctions-imposed-on-russia-by-actor/

Swift, Rocky, and Yuka Obayashi, "Explainer: Why Japan's Power Sector Depends So Much on LNG," Reuters, March 9, 2022.

Tanida, Kuniichi, "Examining Japan's Afghanistan Evacuation Operations," Nippon.com, December 9, 2021.

Timmins, Beth, "Ukraine Airspace Closed to Civilian Flights," BBC, February 24, 2022.

Tocci, Nathalie, "Taiwan Has Learned a Lot from the War in Ukraine—It's Time Europe Caught Up," *Politico*, December 20, 2022.

Tokuchi Hideshi, "What to Do About Japan's Defense Capabilities: What to Consider in Formulating a New National Security Strategy" ["日本の防衛力整備をどうするのか一新たな国家安全保障戦略の策定に向けて考えるべきこと"], Nippon.com, September 13, 2022.

"Ukraine's Coal Imports Up 18% in Q1'2021," *The Coal Hub*, undated.

"Ukraine's Coal Imports Down 67% in Jan–Aug 2022," *The Coal Hub*, undated.

UN—*See* United Nations.

United Nations Development Programme and World Bank, *Ukraine Energy Damage Assessment: Executive Summary*, March 2023.

UN Refugee Agency, "Ukraine Emergency," webpage, undated. As of June 15, 2023:
https://www.unrefugees.org/emergencies/ukraine/

U.S. Energy Information Administration, "Taiwan," webpage, last updated December 2016. As of June 23, 2023:
https://www.eia.gov/international/analysis/country/TWN

U.S. Energy Information Administration, "Japan," webpage, November 2, 2020. As of June 26, 2023:
https://www.eia.gov/international/analysis/country/jpn.

U.S. Energy Information Administration, "Ukraine," webpage, last updated August 2021. As of June 15, 2023:
https://www.eia.gov/international/overview/country/UKR

U.S. Transportation Command, "Support to Allies and Partners in Europe," undated.

Walt, Steven, "The Top 5 Lessons from Year One of Ukraine's War," *Foreign Policy*, February 9, 2023.

Wang, Lisa, "Energy Supplies Sufficient, Ministry Says," *Taipei Times*, August 4, 2022.

"What's Next for Oil and Gas Prices as Sanctions on Russia Intensify," J.P. Morgan, March 10, 2022.

Wong, Chun Han, "China Insists Party Elites Shed Overseas Assets, Eyeing Western Sanctions on Russia," *Wall Street Journal*, May 19, 2022.

World Bank, "GDP (Current US$)," webpage, last updated 2021. As of June 26, 2023:
https://data.worldbank.org/indicator/NY.GDP.MKTP.CD?name_desc=true

World Integrated Trade System (World Bank), "China, Exports and Imports," webpage, last updated 2020. As of June 26, 2023:
https://wits.worldbank.org/CountryProfile/en/Country/CHN/Year/2020/TradeFlow/EXPIMP/Partner/by-country

Worldometer, "Japan Coal," webpage, last updated 2016. As of June 23, 2023:
https://www.worldometers.info/coal/japan-coal/

Worldometer, "Taiwan Coal," webpage, last updated 2016. As of June 23, 2023: https://www.worldometers.info/coal/taiwan-coal/

Wuthnow, Joel, "Rightsizing Chinese Military Lessons from Ukraine," *Strategic Forum*, Center for the Study of Chinese Military Affairs, Institute for National Strategic Studies, National Defense University, September 2022.

Yip, Hilton, "Taiwan Is Rethinking Defense in Wake of Ukraine Invasion," *Foreign Policy*, February 28, 2022.

Zhang, Tiejun, "China Is Not Russia; Taiwan Is Not Ukraine," *The Diplomat*, July 25, 2022.